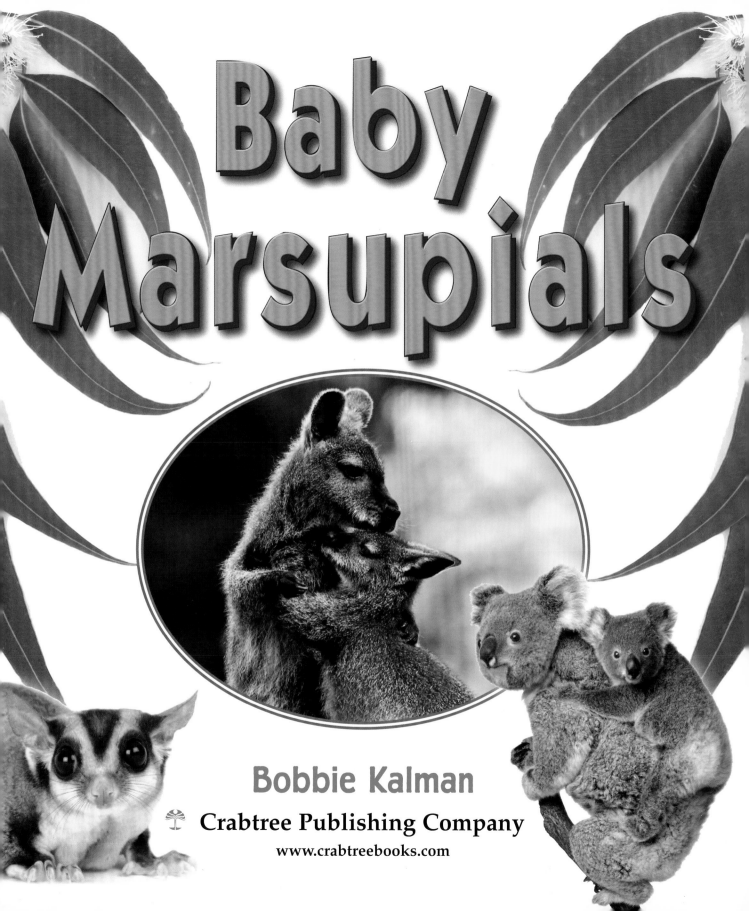

Baby Marsupials

Bobbie Kalman

🌱 Crabtree Publishing Company

www.crabtreebooks.com

It's fun to learn about Baby Animals

Created by Bobbie Kalman

For Aiden Paul Bernard
You are the best big brother ever!
Liam loves you.

**Author and
Editor-in-Chief**
Bobbie Kalman

Editors
Kathy Middleton
Crystal Sikkens

Photo research
Bobbie Kalman

Design
Bobbie Kalman
Katherine Berti
Samantha Crabtree
(logo and front cover)

Print and production coordinator
Katherine Berti

Prepress technician
Katherine Berti

Illustrations
Barbara Bedell: pages 7, 21, 22 (top)
Vanessa Parson-Robbs: page 19
Bonna Rouse: pages 4, 15, 22 (center), 24

Photographs
BigStockPhoto: pages 11 (top), 12 (right), 21, 24 (pouch)
iStockphoto: pages 1 (center), 7 (bottom right), 16, 24 (opossums)
Wikimedia Commons: Geoff Shaw (Zoology, University of
      Melbourne, Australia)/http://kangaroo.genome.org.au:
      page 6 (left); Alan Couch: page 23 (top right)
All other images by Shutterstock

Library and Archives Canada Cataloguing in Publication

Kalman, Bobbie
      Baby marsupials / Bobbie Kalman.

(It's fun to learn about baby animals)
Includes index.
Issued also in electronic format.
ISBN 978-0-7787-4074-2 (bound).--ISBN 978-0-7787-4079-7 (pbk.)

      1. Marsupials--Juvenile literature. 2. Animals--Infancy--Juvenile
literature. I. Title. II. Series: It's fun to learn about baby animals.

QL737.M3K32 2012   j599.2   C2011-907664-0

Library of Congress Cataloging-in-Publication Data

Kalman, Bobbie.
      Baby marsupials / Bobbie Kalman.
            p. cm. -- (It's fun to learn about baby animals)
      Includes index.
      ISBN 978-0-7787-4074-2 (reinforced library binding : alk. paper) --
ISBN 978-0-7787-4079-7 (pbk. : alk. paper) -- ISBN 978-1-4271-7886-2
(electronic pdf) -- ISBN 978-1-4271-8001-8 (electronic html)
      1. Marsupials--Infancy--Juvenile literature. I. Title.

QL737.M3K356 2012
599.2--dc23
                                                            2011046086

Crabtree Publishing Company
www.crabtreebooks.com   1-800-387-7650

Printed in Canada/012012/MA20111130

Published in Canada
Crabtree Publishing
616 Welland Ave.
St. Catharines, Ontario
L2M 5V6

Published in the United States
Crabtree Publishing
PMB 59051
350 Fifth Avenue, 59th Floor
New York, New York 10118

Published in the United Kingdom
Crabtree Publishing
Maritime House
Basin Road North, Hove
BN41 1WR

Published in Australia
Crabtree Publishing
3 Charles Street
Coburg North
VIC 3058

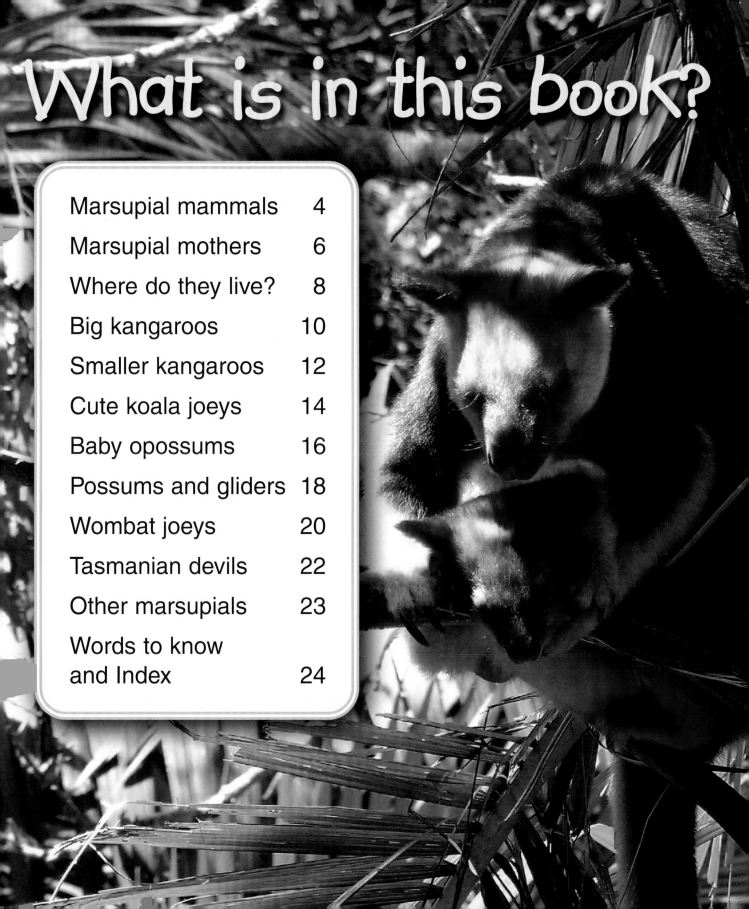

What is in this book?

Marsupial mammals

Marsupials are **mammals**. Most mammals have hair or fur covering their bodies. They are **warm-blooded**. The bodies of warm-blooded animals stay about the same temperature in both warm and cold places. Mammals have **backbones**. A backbone is a row of bones in the middle of an animal's back. All the bones in the body make up the **skeleton**.

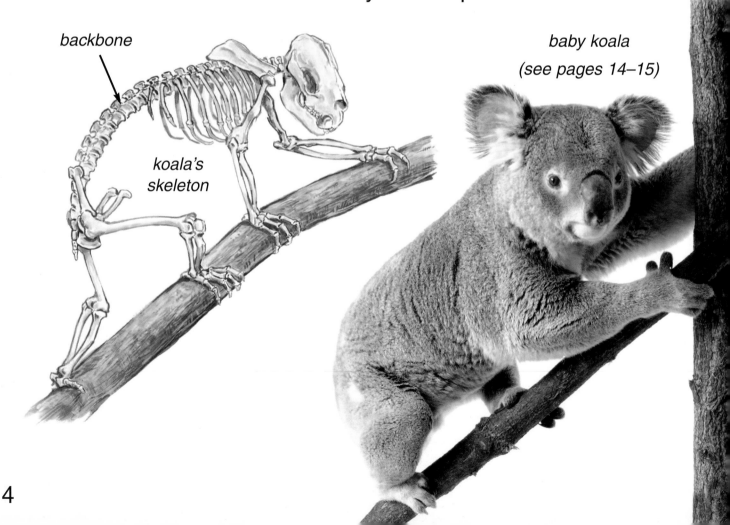

backbone

koala's skeleton

baby koala
(see pages 14–15)

Marsupial babies

The baby animals on this page are **marsupials**. Marsupial babies are called **joeys**. Like other baby mammals, joeys are born. On pages 6–7, find out how they are different from other mammals.

kangaroo joey (see pages 10–11)

Tasmanian devil joey
(see page 22)

wombat joey
(see pages 20–21)

wallaby joey
(see page 12)

opossum joey (see pages 16–17)

sugar glider joey (see page 19)

Marsupial mothers

Most mammal babies are fully developed before they are born, but marsupial joeys are not fully developed. They are tiny and could not live without their mothers. Most marsupial mothers have a **pouch**, or pocket, on their bodies where the babies continue to grow after they are born. Like other mammal babies, joeys **nurse**, or drink milk that is made in the bodies of their mothers. They stay in the pouch for weeks or months before they are ready to come out.

teats

joey

*This kangaroo joey is nursing inside its mother's pouch. It is attached to one of her **teats**. Milk comes through the teats.*

pouch

This kangaroo is peeking out of the pouch at the front of its mother's body.

koala joey in a pouch

A kangaroo's pouch is at the front of the kangaroo's body. A koala's pouch opens toward the bottom and faces outward.

A quokka's pouch is at the front of the mother's body.

Some marsupials do not have deep pouches. An opossum mother, for example, has a small pouch that looks like a flap of skin covering her belly. The joeys above are drinking milk from teats inside the mother's pouch. How many joeys can you count?

Where do they live?

Most marsupials live in Australia and on the nearby islands. The weather in Australia can get very hot, so many marsupials look for food at night, when it is much cooler. Marsupials live in different **habitats**. Habitats are the natural places where animals live. Marsupial habitats include **forests**, **grasslands**, and **deserts**.

Australia

- forests
- grasslands
- deserts

Forests are habitats with many trees. Koalas live in eucalyptus forests. They eat the leaves of eucalyptus trees.

*Tree kangaroos live in **rain forests**. Rain forests are forests that get a lot of rain.*

Kangaroos are found all across Australia. Most live in grasslands. Grasslands are grassy areas with bushes. Kangaroos **graze**, or feed on grasses and small plants. They feed in the mornings and evenings.

Wombats live on grasslands, mountains, and in forests along the edges of oceans.

Some smaller kinds of kangaroos, such as these wallabies, live in deserts.

9

Big Kangaroos

Kangaroos are animals called **macropods**. "Macropod" means "large foot." Kangaroos have strong hind legs, large feet for leaping, and a long tail for balancing. The two biggest kinds of kangaroos are red kangaroos and gray kangaroos. The kangaroo below is a red kangaroo. The macropods on the opposite page are gray kangaroos.

Kangaroos have big feet and a strong tail and legs. Male kangaroos do not have pouches.

long tail

strong legs

big feet

*A kangaroo joey does not leave its mother's pouch for six to eight months. At about six months, the joey starts leaving the pouch for a few minutes at a time but continues to nurse. At about nine months, the joey leaves the pouch for good. This six-month-old joey is nursing from outside the pouch. The joey is an **albino** gray kangaroo. Albino animals are born without color in their fur. They are white.*

*Kangaroos eat mainly plants such as grass, leaves, and roots. Animals that eat mainly plants are called **herbivores**. When this joey stops nursing, it will also eat what its mother eats.*

Smaller kangaroos

Quokkas, wallabies, and tree kangaroos belong to the macropod family, but they are much smaller than red and gray kangaroos. They all carry their joeys in pouches.

A quokka is a chubby kangaroo that is about the size of a pet cat. This little kangaroo can climb small trees and bushes. Like other kangaroos, the quokka is a herbivore.

Wallabies are bigger than quokkas but smaller than red and gray kangaroos. This wallaby is showing where her joey lives.

Tree kangaroos live in trees. They have longer front legs and shorter hind feet than the kangaroos that live on the ground. During the day, tree kangaroos sleep in trees. This kangaroo mother and joey are sleeping. Her joey's head is peeking out of the pouch.

Cute koala joeys

Koala joeys live and grow inside the pouches of their mothers for six months before they come out. Outside the pouch, a young joey clings to its mother's chest. An older joey rides on its mother's back while she climbs, eats, or sleeps. A joey drinks its mother's milk, but it eats a food called **pap**, too. The pap is made in the mother's body. It contains eucalyptus leaves that the mother has eaten.

A koala joey is born blind and deaf. It pulls itself across its mother's belly to her pouch, using its front legs. It attaches itself to a teat inside the pouch and nurses there for six months.

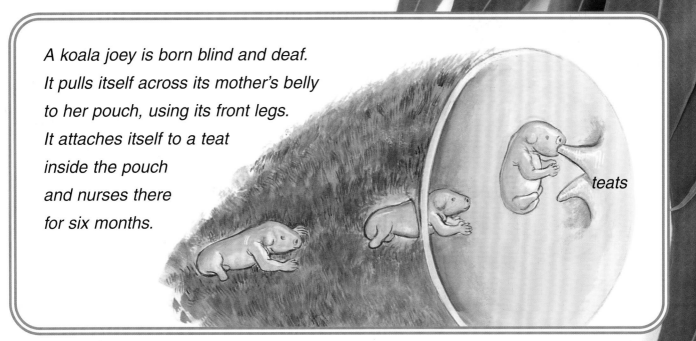

teats

A young joey is hanging on to its mother's chest.

Koalas sleep 16 to 20 hours a day to save **energy**, or strength. Their food does not provide them with much energy.

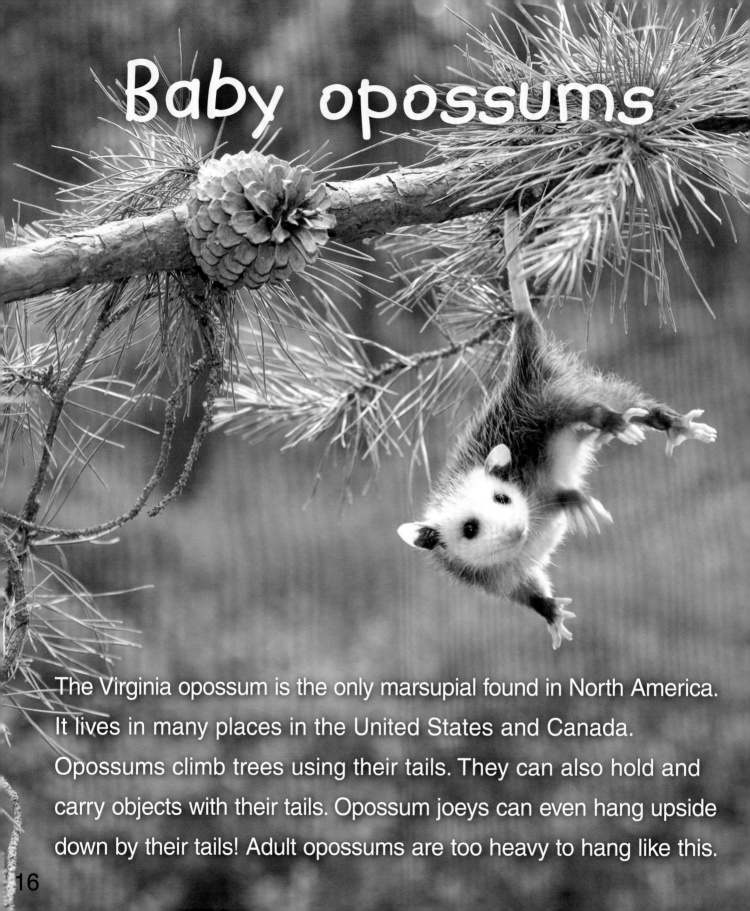

Baby opossums

The Virginia opossum is the only marsupial found in North America. It lives in many places in the United States and Canada. Opossums climb trees using their tails. They can also hold and carry objects with their tails. Opossum joeys can even hang upside down by their tails! Adult opossums are too heavy to hang like this.

Opossum feet

Opossums spend most of their time in trees. On each of their hind feet, they have an inside toe that bends like a thumb. It can touch any other toe. Having feet that work like hands is very helpful for climbing.

This joey is climbing on a deck in someone's back yard. It is looking for fruit, insects, worms, or people's leftover foods to eat. An opossum eats dead animals, too.

Female opossums often give birth to many joeys, but not all can survive. Older joeys hang on to the backs of their mothers until they can live on their own.

Possums and gliders

Possums are not the same as opossums. Possums live in Australia and on nearby islands. They live mainly in trees. There are about 70 kinds of possums. Some eat plants, and others eat both plants and animals. A few eat only eucalyptus leaves. Some feed on **nectar**, a sweet liquid found in flowers, and **pollen**, a fine powder also in flowers.

This common brushtail possum is carrying her joey on her back. After feeding and growing for about five months in the pouch, the joey spends another two months clinging to its mother's back. By the age of seven months, a possum joey can live on its own. Common brushtail possums eat any plants they find. They eat fruit, flowers, eucalyptus leaves, and seeds of all kinds.

Gliding through air

Gliders are related to possums, but they move in different ways. A glider has a furry flap of skin between its front and back legs. The flap allows the animal to glide when it stretches its legs far apart. The wind carries the glider from one tree to another. The gliders on this page are called sugar gliders.

skin flap used for gliding

This four-month-old glider joey has left its mother's pouch. It is finding food on its own. Sugar gliders are active at night. They hunt insects, but they also feed on sweet sap from eucalyptus and acacia trees. They feed on nectar and pollen and sweet fruits, too.

19

Wombat joeys

Wombats are short, chubby marsupials. A wombat joey remains in its mother's pouch nursing and growing for about eight months. One to three months after that, the joey no longer lives in the pouch but continues to drink milk from its mother for up to fifteen months.

*Wombats live in **burrows**. A burrow is an underground home with long tunnels.*

Wombat food

A wombat joey also eats food that its mother helps it find. Wombats eat mainly tough, dry grasses and roots. Their strong front teeth never stop growing. Grinding their food keeps their teeth from growing too long.

This young wombat is looking for plants to eat. It has sharp front teeth.

In their burrows, wombat joeys are safe from **predators**. Predators are animals that hunt and eat other animals. The joeys that have left their pouches stay close to their mothers when they look for food. This joey is hiding behind its mother for protection. Most joeys stay with their mothers for about two years.

A wombat's paw is flat and wide and has long, curved claws for digging burrows.

A wombat mother's pouch faces backward, so when she is digging, her joey will not get dirty.

Tasmanian devils

Tasmanian devils were named for their scary looks and loud screams. These marsupials are found in all habitats in Tasmania, an island that is part of Australia. Mother devils have two to three joeys at a time. The joeys leave the pouch completely at about three months of age. They stay in their mother's **den**, or home, for three more months.

Tasmanian devils have strong jaws and sharp teeth. They eat both plants and other animals.

Devils sometimes stomp their feet and jump from side to side to scare away other animals.

This Tasmanian devil's den is a hole in the ground.

Other marsupials

Many marsupials are herbivores. Some marsupials are **carnivores**. Carnivores eat other animals, such as insects and lizards. **Omnivores** eat both plants and animals.

Planigales are the smallest marsupials. They are predators that hunt and eat insects and small lizards.

Bilbies eat insects, seeds, and mushrooms. They are omnivores.

Numbats are carnivores that eat ants and termites. They do not have pouches for their joeys.

Quolls are predators. They have spots on their fur that blend in with their habitat. Spots help quolls hide while they are hunting.

23

Words to Know and Index

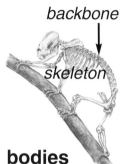

backbone

skeleton

bodies
pages 4, 6,
7, 14, 17

food
pages 8, 9,
11, 14, 15, 17,
18, 19, 20, 21

gliders
pages 5,
18, 19

kangaroos
pages 5, 6, 7,
8, 9, 10–11,
12, 13

koalas
pages
4, 7, 8,
14–15

opossums
pages 5, 7,
16–17

pouch
pages 6, 7, 10,
11, 12, 13, 14,
15, 18, 19, 20,
21, 22, 23

**Tasmanian
devils**
pages 5, 22

Other index words

wallabies
pages 5, 9, 12

wombats
pages 5, 9, 20–21